Wizard

Materials

Materials:

- Cherry: 1" x 6¼" x 10" (25mm x 159mm x 254mm)

Halfling and Dwarf

Materials

Materials:

- Halfling: Cherry: 1" x 5¼" x 5 ½" (25mm x 133mm x 140mm)
- Dwarf: Cherry: 1" x 4½" x 7¼" (25mm x 114mm x 184mm)

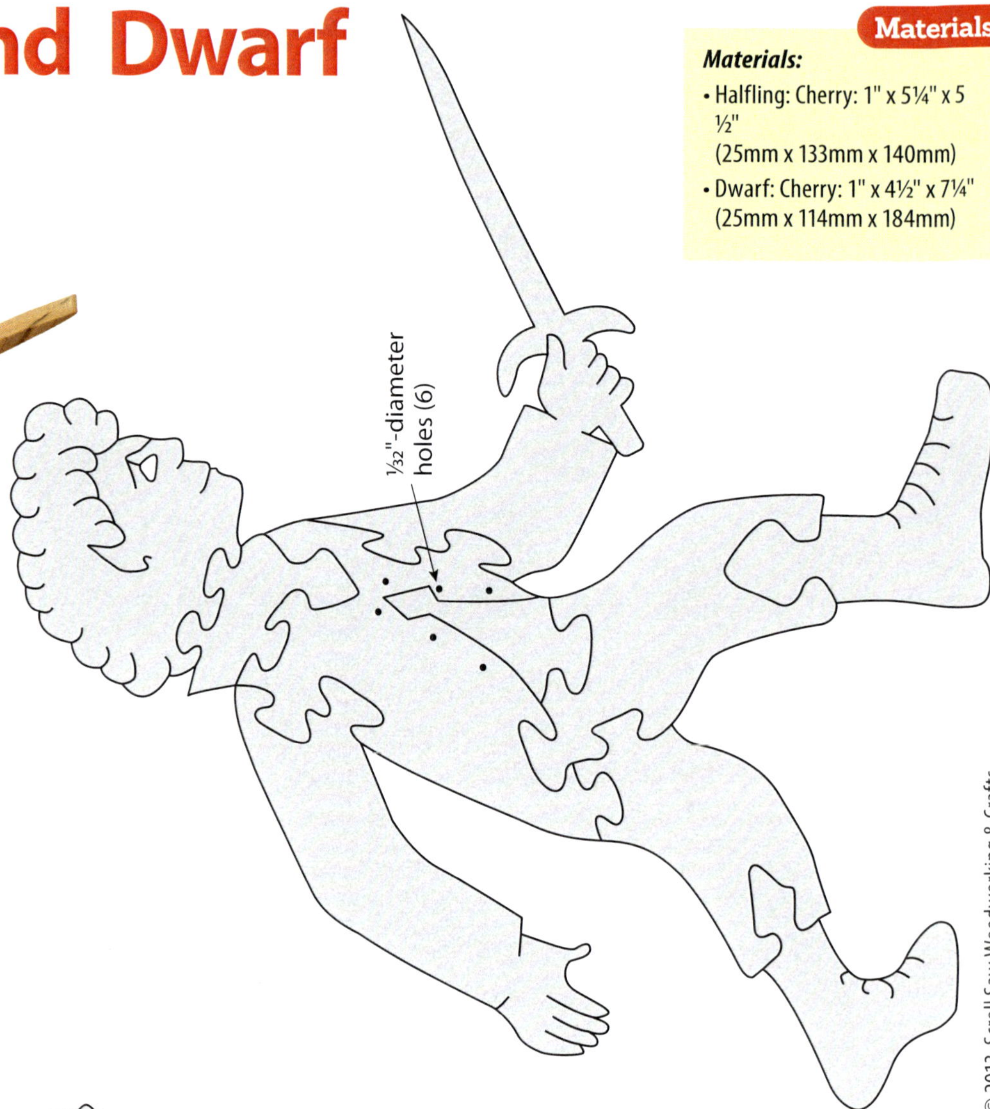

Elf and Elf Lady

Materials

Materials:

- Elf: Cherry: 1" x 4½" x 8½" (25mm x 114mm x 216mm)
- Elf Lady: Maple: 1" x 5" x 7½" (25mm x 127mm x 191mm)

Dragon

Materials

Materials:

- Dragon: Chakte kok: 1" x 6" x 6¾" (25mm x 152mm x 171mm)
- Treasure: Satinwood, 1" x 6" x 6¾" (25mm x 152mm x 171mm)

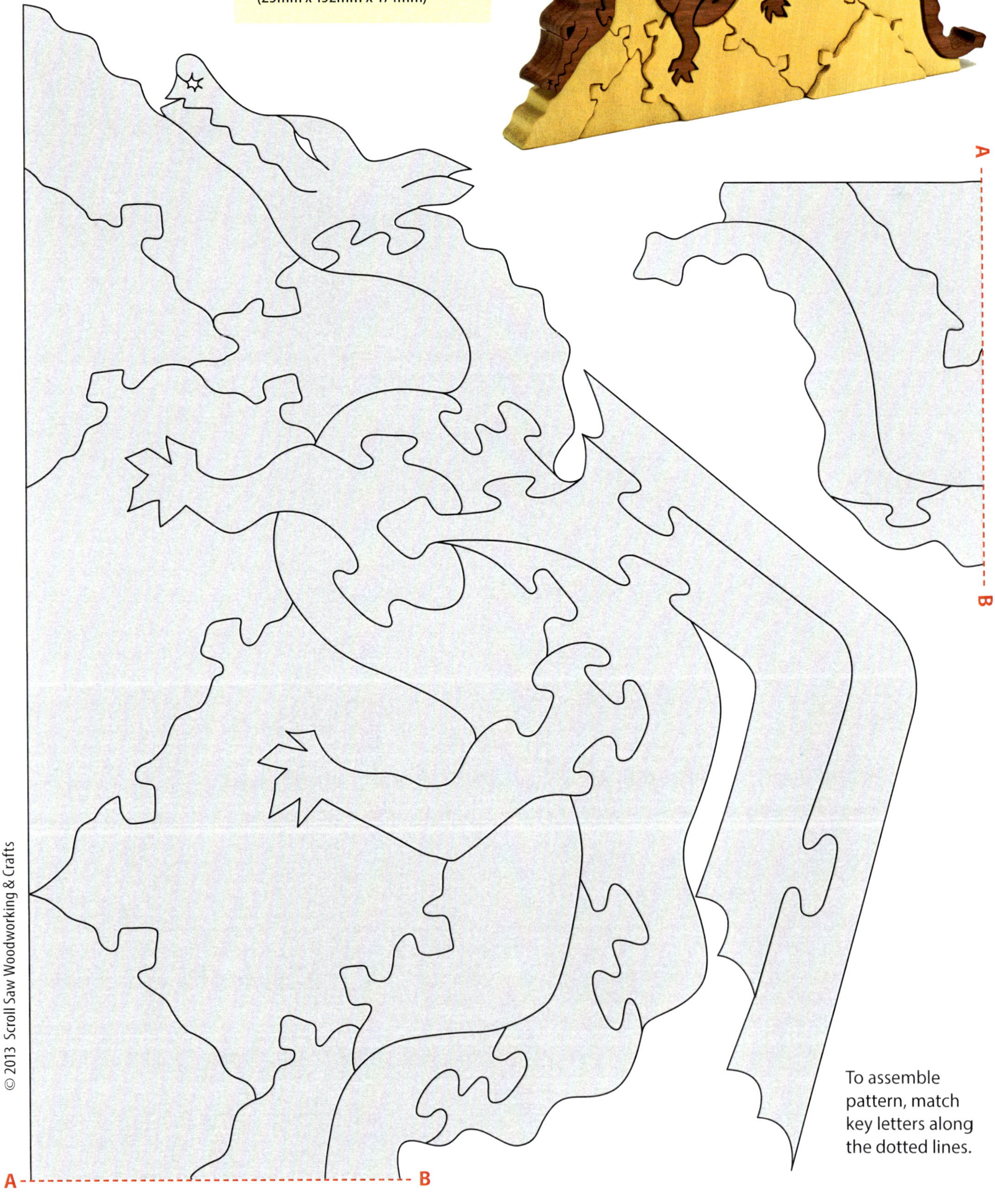

To assemble pattern, match key letters along the dotted lines.

Bear Man

Materials

Materials:

- Sycamore: 1" x 5½" x 9¼" (25mm x 140mm x 235mm)

The Wizard's Ride
(Giant Eagle)

To assemble pattern, match key letters along the dotted lines. Align the A-B line first, then the C-D line.

Materials

Materials:

- Cherry: 1" x 15½" x 15½" (25mm x 394mm x 394mm)

Goblin

Materials

Materials:

- Walnut: 1" x 6" x 9½" (25mm x 152mm x 241mm)

Troll

Materials

Materials:

- Butternut*: 1⅜" x 3¾" x 6½" (35mm x 95mm x 165mm)

Drill nostrils with ¹⁄₁₆" (2mm) bit

*I chose the ugliest piece of wood I've ever seen—it seemed appropriate for a troll.

Giant Spider

To turn the body on a lathe:

Determine the center of the blank, and then measure down ½" (13mm) from the center and make a mark. Chuck the blank in the lathe on the mark and turn the shape of the body. Because the blank is offset, the bottom will remain flat while you round and shape the top and sides.

To make the body with a saw:

Attach the compound cutting pattern to a corner of the blank. Cut one side, tape the waste in place, and cut the second side. You may need to use a band saw to cut the thick material. Remove the pattern and waste wood, and carve and/or sand off the sharp corners.

To complete the spider:

Use a ⅛" (3mm) bit to drill ½" (13mm)-deep holes for the legs in the bottom of the body. Cut the legs and mandibles, and use the ⅛" (3mm) bit to drill holes as indicated for the dowels. Glue a 1" (25mm)-long piece of ⅛" (3mm) dowel into each leg and a ¾" (19mm)-long piece into each mandible. Then, use Behlen's jet black dye to color all of the pieces (use the zipper bag method). Allow the dye to dry for 24 hours and then seal the pieces with natural Danish oil. Allow the Danish oil to dry.

For the eyes, refer to the face diagram and use ⅛" (3mm) and ⅓₂" (1mm) bits to drill indentions as marked to form the sockets. Switch to a #70 bit to drill a ½" (13mm)-deep hole in each indention. Use red polymer clay to mold six ⅛" (3mm) and two ¼" (6mm) eyes around the heads of straight pins (make extras). Bake the clay on a ceramic tile according to the manufacturer's instructions. Allow the clay to cool, cut the pins off at ½" (13mm), and push them into place.

To keep the spider as a puzzle, as well as maintain poseability, press-fit the legs and mandibles into place but do not glue them.

Materials & Tools

Materials:

- Body, dyed pine: 1½" x 3" x 6½" (38mm x 76mm x 165mm);
- Legs, dyed pine: ⅜" x 6½" x 10" (10mm x 165mm x 254mm); Mandibles, pine, ¼" x 1" x 1" (6mm x 25mm x 25mm)

Additional tools:

- Lathe and turning tools OR band saw, carving tools, and sanding tools
- Drill bits: ⅛", ⅓₂", #70 (or size to match straight pin)
- Oven
- Ceramic tile
- Wire cutters

Additional materials:

- Dowel*: ⅛" dia. x 8" (3mm x 203mm)
- Dye: Behlen's jet black
- Straight pins: 15 each
- Polymer clay: red
- Cyanoacrylate (CA) glue

*Note: Dyeing the dowel can weaken it. Consider soaking the dowel in thinned CA glue and letting it dry before using it.

The author used these products for the project. Substitute your choice of brands, tools, and materials as desired.

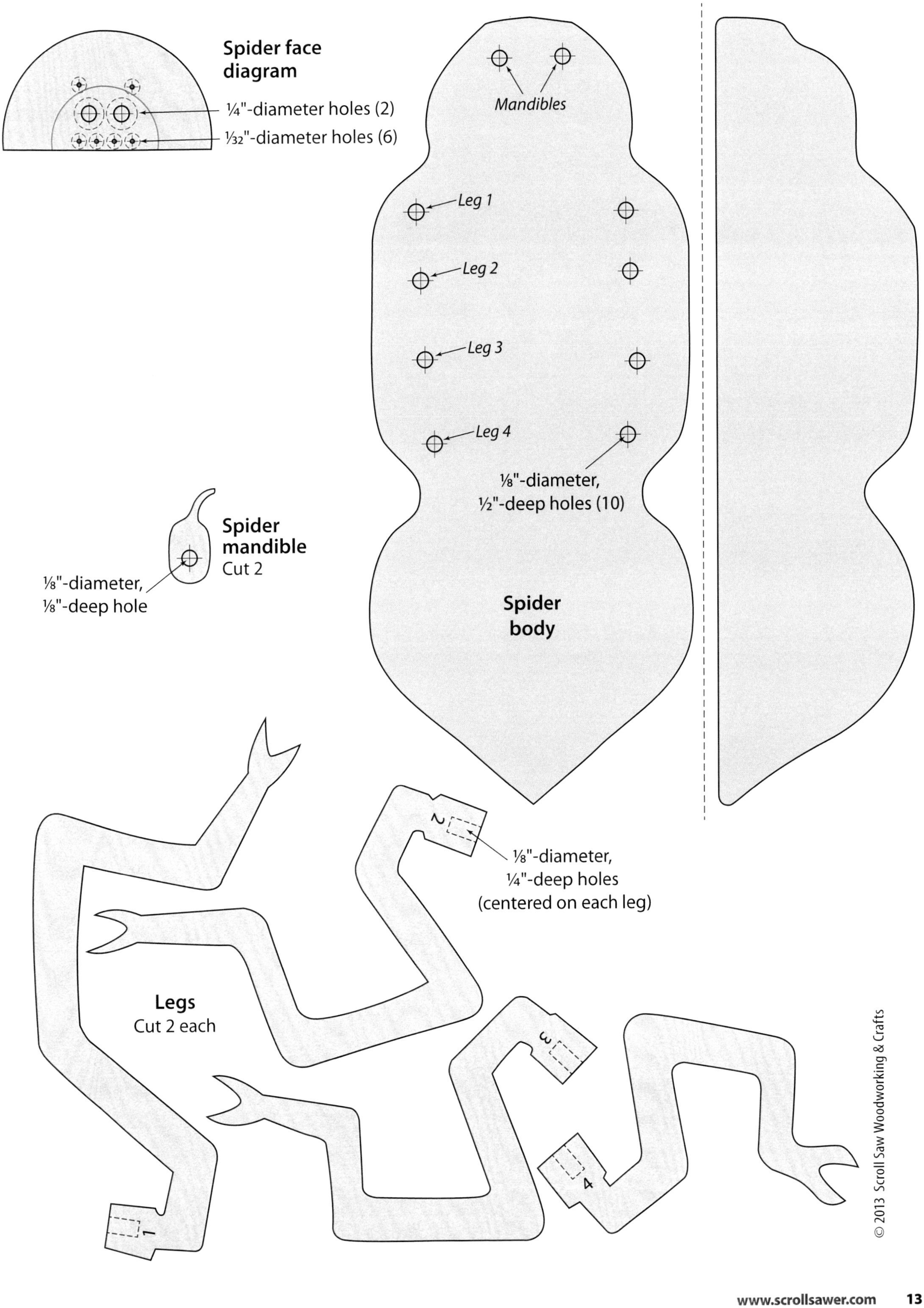
Spider face diagram
¼"-diameter holes (2)
1⁄32"-diameter holes (6)
Mandibles
Leg 1
Leg 2
Leg 3
Leg 4
⅛"-diameter, ½"-deep holes (10)
Spider mandible
Cut 2
⅛"-diameter, ⅛"-deep hole
Spider body
⅛"-diameter, ¼"-deep holes (centered on each leg)
Legs
Cut 2 each
1
2
3
4

Dire Wolf (Warg) and Tortured Soul

Materials

Materials:

- Warg: Walnut: 1" x 3¾" x 8¾" (25mm x 95mm x 222mm
- Tortured Soul: Walnut: 1" x 3¼" x 5¾" (25mm x 83mm x 146mm)

Drill eyes with 1⁄16" (2mm) bit.

Drill nostrils with 1⁄32" (1mm) bit.

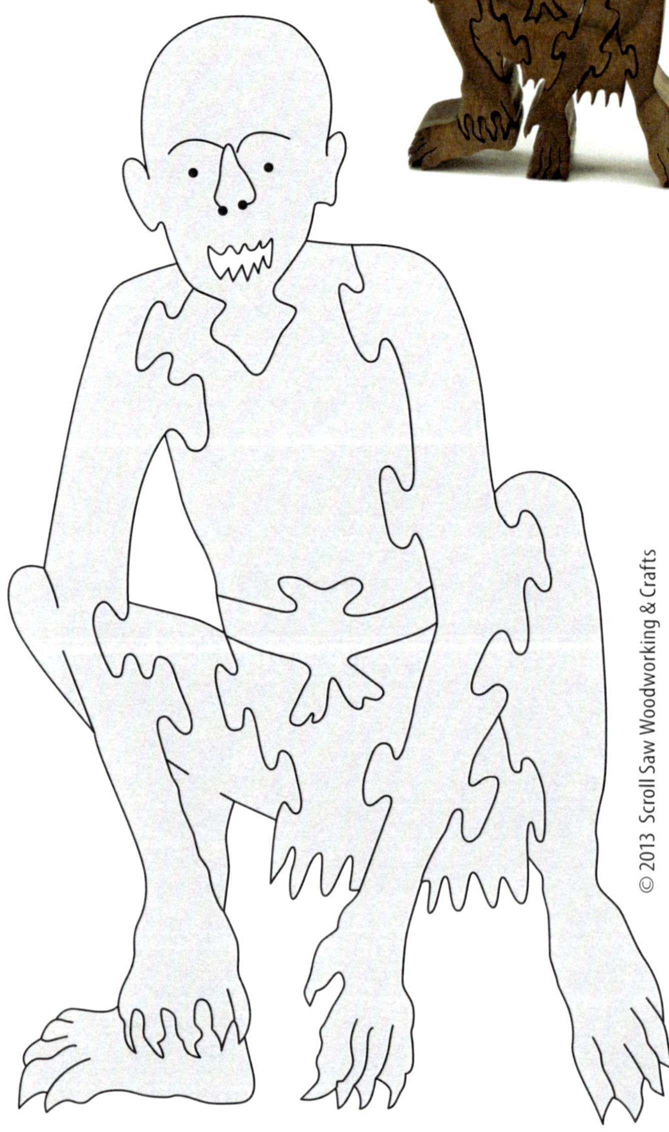